## Zauberhafte Bergwelt
# ALLGÄU

# ZIETHEN-PANORAMA VERLAG

DIETER SEIBERT

## Zauberhafte Bergwelt
# ALLGÄU

Allgäu – das Wort leitet sich von Alp-Gau her. Man hat hier – zumindest im südlichen Teil – schon vor einer regelrechten Besiedelung das Vieh zum Sömmern, eben auf die Alp, getrieben. Später gewannen die Klöster große Bedeutung, etwa das um 750 gegründete Kloster St. Magnus in Füssen. Von ihnen ging die Urbarmachung weiter Regionen aus. Doch nie wurde das Allgäu zum selbständigen Land, zu einem eigenen Staatswesen. So fehlen feste Grenzen, etwa gegenüber dem nördlich anschließenden Bayerisch-Schwaben oder im Nordwesten gegen das württembergische Oberschwaben.

Selbst die Einheimischen lassen sich nicht exakt einer Volksgruppe zuordnen. Im Süden sind es Alemannen, also Verwandte der Vorarlberger und Schweizer. Aber es gibt gegen Norden keine klare Abgrenzung zu den Schwaben. Ein Tip für den Gast zu diesem Thema: wer es sich mit der ansässigen Bevölkerung nicht verderben will, sollte sie nie mit den Württemberger Schwaben über einen Kamm scheren. Allgäuer sind Allgäuer!

Das Allgäu präsentiert sich fast überall als weite, freie, wiesenreiche Region voller Sonne, gewissermaßen ein lachendes Land (wenn nicht gerade Regenwolken den Himmel bedecken). Hier prägen nicht dunkle Fichtenwälder das Bild, und selbst die in die Berge ziehenden Täler sind nie eng und düster. Dieses Liebenswerte ist der eigentliche Magnet, der die Gäste so zahlreich ins Allgäu lockt und sie stets wiederkommen läßt. Es gibt gute Gründe für die vielen Wiesenflächen im Vorland und im Tal, für die Alpweiden oben in den Bergen. Milchwirtschaft und Rinderzucht waren hier stets die wesentlichen Erwerbsquellen. Durch das harte Ringen der Bauern über Jahrhunderte wurde aus dem einstigen Urwald die blühende Landschaft von heute.

## The Magical World of
# ALLGÄU
### Mountains

Allgäu - the word is derived from Alp-Gau (Alpine province) - was an area, at least the southern part, where the cattle were driven to alpine pastures in the summer, even before the area was properly settled. Later the monasteries grew important, for example the St. Magnus monastery in Füssen, founded about 750. They proceeded to cultivate further regions. Yet the Allgäu was never an independent territory, with its own political autonomy. Thus there are no fixed borders with Bavarian Swabia to the north or the Upper Swabian part of Württemberg in the northwest.

Even the population cannot be assigned precisely to a particular ethnic group. In the south there are Alemannians, related to the populace of the Vorarlberg and Switzerland. But in the north there is no clear demarcation between the inhabitants of the Allgäu and the Swabians. A tip for visitors: you'll put your foot in it if you ever suggest the people of the Allgäu are one with the Swabians of Württemberg. Allgäuer are Allgäuer!

The Allgäu is, nearly everywhere, a broad, open region of meadows, sunny, in a word a smiling landscape (at least as long as the sky is not full of rain clouds). Dark pine forests and narrow, gloomy valleys are uncharacteristic. It is the light, endearing nature of the countryside that is the real magnet, drawing visitors in such large numbers to the Allgäu, again and again. There are good reasons for the numerous meadowlands in the foothills and the valleys, for the Alpine pastures high up in the mountains. Dairy and cattle farming have always been the main source of livelihood. The flourishing landscape of today is the result of a tenacious, centuries-long struggle between farmers and the virgin forest.

## Viaggio illustrato a colori attraverso
# L'ALGOV

Allgäu - la parola deriva da Alp-Gau, cioè da pascolo alpino in quanto almeno nella parte meridionale si è condotto il bestiame all'alpeggio già prima che ci fossero dei veri insediamenti. Dopo anche i monasteri conquistarono una grande importanza come per esempio il convento di St. Magno a Füssen, fondato verso il 750. Su loro iniziativa il terreno fu bonificato. Ma l'Algovia non diventò mai uno stato indipendente e così mancano le frontiere ben definite verso il Bayrisch-Schwaben al nord e l'Oberschwaben al nord-ovest.

Persino gli abitanti con appartengono chiaramente a un gruppo etnico. Al sud sono alemanni, quindi parenti degli svizzeri e del Vorarlberg. Ma al nord non c'è una dinstizione tra loro e gli svevi del Baden-Württemberg. Un piccolo avviso per gli ospiti: Per non fare brutta figura, non confondere gli svevi dell'Algovia con quelli del Baden-Württemberg. La gente dell'Algovia rimane dell'Algovia!

L'Algovia si presenta quasi dappertutto come regione ampia, libera e piena di prati e sole, una regione sorridente (se non ci sono nuvole piovose). Non ci sono foreste di abeti scure e anche le vallate delle montagne non sono mai strette o buie. E questo il magneta che attrae ogni anni tanti visitatori e che li fa tornare sempre. Che ci siano tanti prati sia in pianura che in montagna ha una buona ragione. L'industria casearia e l'allevamento di bovini rappresentano da sempre la fonte di guadagno più importante. Attraverso il centenario lavoro duro dei contadini la giungla di allora è diventata la regione fiorita di oggi. Per avere più prati e pascoli possibili, si è spinto indietro di molto la foresta.

Um so viele Mähwiesen und Weiden wie nur irgend möglich zu schaffen, drängte man den Wald weiter und weiter zurück. Die ungewöhnliche Höhe des Allgäus – auch außerhalb der Alpen gibt es Dörfer und Höfe, die höher als 1000 m liegen, etwa Diepolz (1037 m) oder Mittelberg (1035 m) – macht zudem den Ackerbau weitgehend unrentabel; so herrscht hier fast überall das helle Grün der Wiesen. Es ist also wohlbegründet, dass die Region neben ihrer Bedeutung als Ferien-Dorado noch heute als Butter- und Käseland in ganz Deutschland bekannt ist.

Wir wollen bei der folgenden Farbbild-Rundreise mit zwei recht unterschiedlichen Hälften das Allgäu in all seinen Facetten kennenlernen. Der Nordbogen führt durch das Alpenvorland, und die lange Kette der Berge füllt nur wie ein Scherenschnitt den Horizont im Süden. Manche Kirche des Barock und Rokoko, darunter wertvolle Kleinode wie Ottobeuren, lädt zu einem Besuch. Klöster, Schlösser, Burgen und Ruinen erinnern an eine Kleinstaaterei, wie es sie kaum in einer anderen Region in so extremer Weise gegeben hat. So lag und liegt manchmal ein katholisches Dorf unmittelbar neben einem evangelischen. Zum Allgäuer „Fleckerlteppich" tragen natürlich auch die einstigen Freien Reichsstädte bei, etwa Wangen, Leutkirch, Memmingen, Kaufbeuren . Viel Historisches blieb erhalten oder wurde kunstgerecht restauriert; so gehört ein Bummel durch die von Leben pulsierenden Altstädte, verbunden mit einem Besuch im gemütlichen Straßencafé, zu den bleibenden Eindrücken. Doch vor lauter Historie sollte niemand die Umgebung vergessen, dieses oft noch stille, ursprüngliche Bauernland inmitten von Hügeln, Seen, Weihern, Mooren …

In order to create as many hay meadows and pastures as they could, the forests were made to retreat further and further. The unusually high altitude - even outside the Alpine region there are villages and farms that are over 1000m up, for example Diepolz (1037m) or Mittelberg (1035m) - made arable farming largely uneconomic anyway. So everywhere the bright green of the meadows predominates. So it is not without reason that the area is known not just as a holidaymaker's Eldorado, but also all over Germany as a land of butter and cheese.

On the following pictorial tour we shall get to know the Allgäu in all its richness from two quite different sides. The northern sweep takes us through the alpine foothills, the long chain of mountains silently filling the horizon in the south like a silhouette. Many a baroque and rococo church, including such jewels as Ottobeuren, will invite us to stop and tarry. Monasteries, castles, fortresses and ruins are a reminder of particularism, with miniature states on a scale more extreme than in any other region. Thus a catholic village might lie, and still lies immediately next to a protestant one. The former free imperial towns are also an integral part of the bright Allgäu quilt, Wangen, Leutkirch, Memmingen, Kaufbeuren etc. Many historical remains have been preserved or skilfully restored: a stroll through the pulsating streets of the old towns, combined with a leisurely visit to a street cafe leaves lasting impressions. Yet all the history should not be allowed to overshadow the surrounding countryside, the still very peaceful, unspoilt farming landscape in the midst of hills, lakes, ponds and moorland …

L'altezza notevole dell'Algovia - anche al di fuori delle Alpi ci sono paesi con altezze di più di 1000 metri, come Diepolz (1037) o Mittelberg (1035) rende l'agricoltura non redditizia; quindi regge il verde dei prati e pascoli. Si capisce che l'Algovia oltre a essere una meta di vacanze è conosciuta come regione del formaggio e del burro.

Durante il seguente viaggio illustrato da foto a colori diviso in due parti, conosceremo l'Algovia con tutti i suoi particolari. A nord c'è l'altopiano ai piedi del versante settentrionale delle Alpi e la lunga catena di montagne a sud completa il paesaggio incantevole. Alcune chiese del barocco o del rococò, tra esse preziosi gioielli come Ottobeuren invitano i visitatori. Monasteri, castelli, fortezze e rovine fanno ricordare l'era dei piccolissimi stati come in nessun'altra regione. Ancora oggi si trovano paesi cattolici e protestanti in diretta vicinanza. Fanno parte della svarietazza dell'Algovia anche le vecchie libere città dell'impero come Wangen, Leutkirch, Memmingen, Kaufbeuren e così via. Molte costruzioni storiche si sono conservate o furono restaurate; una passeggiata per i centri storici pieni di vita, un caffè in un bar in piazza rimarranno sempre in mente dei visitatori. Ma nonostante la ricchezza storica non bisogna mai dimenticare di godere il paesaggio pacifico e naturale nel mezzo di colline, laghi, laghetti e paludi....

Il nostro viaggio ci porterà poi al sud dell'Algovia con tutti i monumenti che lo hanno reso conosciuto, la Wieskirche, il castello Neuschwanstein e la metropoli di Kempten per poi arrivare al centro di sport alpino Obertsdorf. L'Algovia orientale è una delle regioni più belle di tutto l'altopiano con sei grandi laghi e circa venti laghetti idillici che danno tutti su cantene di montagne impressionanti. Non dimentichiamo però anche l'impero di re Ludovico II. nel Schwangau!

## FORGGENSEE mit Blick zum Säuling (2047m)

Recht spektakulär kommt der Lech bei Füssen aus Tirol ins Bayerische. Der Lechfall bildet zwar nur eine Stufe von mäßiger Höhe, die erstaunlich reichen Wassermassen dieses Bergflusses sorgen dennoch für ein eindrucksvolles Schauspiel. Gleich am anderen Ende der Stadt ergießt sich der Lech dann in den Forggensee. Er ist der einzige Stausee des Ostallgäus mit 10 km Länge und der größten Wasserfläche, gleich beliebt bei Badenden, Seglern, Surfern und Motorschiff-Ausflüglern.

The Lech enters Bavaria near Füssen from Tyrol quite spectacularly. The waterfall may have only one moderately high section, but the amazingly abundant volume of water ensures an impressive spectacle. At the other end of the town, the Lech pours forth into the Forggensee. This is the only reservoir in the East Allgäu, 10 km long and its largest expanse of water, popular with bathers, sailors, surfers and motorboat-trippers alike.

E uno spettacolo impressionante vedere entrare il fiume Lech a Füssen dal Tirolo alla Baviera con la cascata del Lech. Non sono molte alte le cascate, ma a causa di grandi masse d'acqua sono belle da vedere. Subito dopo dall'altra parte della città il fiume va nel lago Forggensee. E l'unica diga dell'Algovia orientale con 10 chilometri di lunghezza e una superficie molto grande che la rende attraente sia per i bagnanti che per quelli in barca a vela, quelli che fanno il windsurfing o vanno in motonave.

### Fortsetzung der Einleitung

Der Südbogen unserer Rundreise bringt dann all das Berühmte des Allgäus von der Wieskirche über Schloß Neuschwanstein und die Metropole Kempten bis zum Ferien- und Wintersportzentrum Oberstdorf. Zu den schönsten Alpenrand-Landschaften überhaupt zählt das Ostallgäu mit seinen sechs großen Wasserflächen und etwa zwanzig kleinen, oft sehr idyllischen und unberührten Seen und Weihern, die alle vor einer malerisch-markanten Felsgipfel-Kulisse liegen. Und nicht zu vergessen: das Reich des Märchenkönigs Ludwig II. im Schwangau!

Tief in die Berge hinein zieht das breite, waldarme, sehr sonnige Tal der Iller mit seinen Nebentälern. Viele beliebte Ferienziele wie Maria Steinbach, Kempten, Immenstadt, Sonthofen oder Oberstdorf liegen an der Iller. Spazierengehen, wandern, bergsteigen sind die Beschäftigungen der Gäste. Es gibt so viel zum Bewundern, etwa Wildbäche, Wasserfälle, Klammen, Schluchten – hier Tobel genannt – Bergseen, Felswände, man findet so lockende Ziele wie Almen (im Allgäu: Alpen), in denen der Gast mehr als Milch und Butter bekommt, Berghütten, oft mit einer Speisekarte wie in einem Gasthof, Gipfelkreuze und vieles mehr. Zum allgegenwärtigen Bild gehören schließlich die großen Berge mit ihren oft geheimnisvollen, die Phantasie anregenden Namen wie Hochvogel, Mädelegabel, Schneck, Höfats, Daumen, Himmelschrofen, um nur ein paar zu nennen.

### End of the introduction

The southern sweep of our tour encompasses all the famous sights, from the Wieskirche to Neuschwanstein Castle, the metropolis of Kempten and the holiday and winter sports centre, Oberstdorf. The East Allgäu is one of the most beautiful Alpine borderlands, with six large lakes and about twenty often very idyllic unspoilt smaller ones, some no bigger than a pond, all set against a picturesque rocky background. And not to be forgotten, the fairy-tale kingdom of Ludwig II in Schwangau.

The broad, sparsely wooded, sunny valley of the Iller with its side valleys stretches up from Maria Steinbach, via Kempten, Immenstadt, Sonthofen and many other popular holiday resorts high up into the mountains at Oberstdorf. Walking, hiking, climbing are the visitors' pastimes. There is so much to admire: tumbling mountain streams, waterfalls, gorges and ravines - called „Tobel" here - mountain lakes, rockfaces, Alpine pastures where visitors can refresh themselves with more than just milk and butter, mountain huts often with a menu as long as an inn's, crosses on the summits. The picture is rounded off by the omnipresent high mountains with their intriguing, mysterious names such as Hochvogel (High Bird), Mädelegabel (Girls' Fork), Daumen (Thumb) or Schneck (Snail).

### Continuazione dell'introduzione

La valle del fiume Iller si estende fino alle montagne, è larga, molto soleggiata e parte da Maria Steinbach e attraversa Kempten, Immenstadt, Sonthofen e altre cittadine per poi arrivare a Oberstdorf. Passeggiate in pianura o in montagna ecco quello che fanno i numerosi ospiti. C'è tanto da ammirare, fiumicelli, gole, forre (in Algovia Tobel), cascate, laghi alpini, rocce e poi anche i pascoli alpini, chiamati Alpen in Algovia dove l'ospite trova molto più del solito burro e formaggio. Poi ci sono osterie alpine offrendo cibi locali delicati. E infine ci sono le montagne onnipresenti con nomi che ispirano molto la fantasia come Hochvogel, Mädeleabel, Schneck, Höfats, Daumen, Himmelsschrofen per citarne solo alcuni.

**FORGGENSEE mit Schwänen im Sonnenuntergang**

**HOPFENSEE mit Blick zum Säuling im Ostallgäu / East Allgäu / Algovia orientale**

Wasser, Wiesen und eine imposante Bergkulisse bilden den Dreiklang, der das Ostallgäu zu einer der schönsten Alpenrand-Landschaften macht. Zu den sechs großen Wasserflächen zählen der fast unberührte Bannwaldsee und der Hopfensee. Dessen Nordufer, das im Ferien- und Kurort Hopfen bei Füssen liegt, säumt eine richtige Promenade, während im Süden und Westen Schilf, Sumpf und Moore ein Dorado für Wasservögel schaffen. Eine weitere Ostallgäu-Eigenart sind die ungewöhnlich farbkräftigen Sonnenuntergänge.

Water, meadows and an impressive mountain silhouette form the triad that makes the East Allgäu one of the most beautiful landscapes bordering on the Alps. Among the six large expanses of water are the almost unspoilt Bannwaldsee and the Hopfensee. The latter's northern shoreline in the holiday and spa centre Hopfen near Füssen, is bordered by a genuine promenade, while to the south and west reeds, marsh and moor provide an Eldorado for waterfowl. Another special feature of the East Allgäu are the unusually colourful sunsets.

L'acqua, i prati e le montagne imponenti sono le attrazioni che rendono l'Algovia una delle regioni più belle dell'altopiano. Due dei sei laghi sono il Bannwaldsee e il Hopfensee. Sulla riva settentrionale del Hopfensee si trova un bel lungolago che circonda il paese di villeggiatura e bagno termale Hopfen, vicino a Füssen. Sulle rive meridionali ed occidentali si trovano paludi, canne e pantani, un vero paradiso per uccelli acquatici. Un'altra caratteristica dell'Algovia orientale si manifesta nei bellissimi tramonti, pieni di caldi colori.

## 8  BANNWALDSEE / Ostallgäu

Weite Wiesen, fast senkrecht darüber ragt der 2047 m hohe Säuling, das weltberühmte Schloß Neuschwanstein und dazu noch eine sehenswerte Wallfahrtskirche – das gibt es nur im Ostallgäu! St. Coloman ist ein Werk des Wessobrunner Baumeisters Johann Schmuzer.– Ein Ausruf des Erstaunens ist das Übliche beim ersten Blick auf dieses oft geisterhaft wirkende Märchenschloß Neuschwanstein, das etwa 160 m über den Wiesen des Schwangaus vor den felsdurchsetzten Berghängen steht.

## 9  ST. COLOMAN mit Neuschwanstein

Broad meadows, the 2047 metre-high Säuling rising up almost verti-cally above them, the world-famous Neuschwanstein Castle, and on top of that a fine pilgrimage church - you'll only find that in the East Allgäu! St. Coloman was built by the Wessobrunn architect Johann Schmuzer – A cry of astonishment is the usual response to a first sight of this magic, sometimes ghostly, fairytale castle Neuschwanstein, perched 160 metres up above the Schwangau meadowlands against the craggy backdrop of the mountains.

## Die Königsschlösser mit Blick über den Schwangau  10/11

Ampi prati e dietro quasi verticale il monte Säuling (2047 m), il famoso castello di Neuschwanstein e il bellissimo santuario - ecco, sono attrazioni che non si trovano al di fuori dell'Algovia orientale! St. Coloman è un'opera dell'architetto Johann Schmuzer di Wesobrunn. – Quando i visitatori vedono il castello favoloso di Neuschwanstein per la prima volta non possono che esprimere il loro sommo stupore. Si trova a circa 160 metri sopra i prati dello Schwangau davanti alle colline rocciose.

## SCHLOSS NEUSCHWANSTEIN, Sängersaal — Arbeitszimmer König Luwig II. / Study room / Lo studio

Diese „mittelalterliche" Idealburg entstand erst um 1870 nach den Vorstellungen König Ludwig II. von Bayern, der sich in seinen späten Jahren hier in scheuer Zurückgezogenheit gerne aufhielt. Heute defilieren täglich Tausende durch das prunkvolle Innere mit dem Sänger- und dem Thronsaal. Das königliche Arbeitszimmer ist im romanischen Stil, gehalten hier zog sich Ludwig für seine Regierungsgeschäfte zurück. Die Beleuchtungskörper bestehen aus vergoldetem Messing. Die Gemälde des Arbeitszimmers drehen sich alle um das Thema des „Thannhäusers" und den Sängerkrieg auf der Wartburg.

The castle, typifying everything "medieval", was not in fact built until 1870, by King Ludwig II of Bavaria, who liked to retreat here shyly in his later years. Today, thousands file through the resplendent interior daily, with its Singers Gallery and throne room. The royal study is designed in Romanesque style. This is where Ludwig withdrew to deal with affairs of state. The lighting fixtures are made of gilded brass. The paintings in the study revolve round the topic of Thannhäuser and the war of the singers on the Wartburg.

La fortezza ideale di stile "medievale" risale solo al 1870 e fu costruito su ordine di re Ludovico II di Baviera che vi soggiornava spesso e a lungo negli ultimi anni della sua vita. Oggi migliaia di persone vengono tutti i giorni per vedere l'interno opulento con la sala dei cantanti e del trono. Lo studio reale, che ha mantenuto lo stile romanico, è il luogo dove Ludwig si ritirava per sbrigare gli affari del regno. I corpi di illuminazione consistono di ottone dorato. I dipinti dello studio ruotano tutti attorno al tema del "Thannhäuser" e della guerra dei Cantori sulla Wartburg.

## ALPSEE bei Schloss Hohenschwangau

Nur am Osteck des Alpsees stehen ein paar Häuser, über denen ganz nahe und auffallend Schloß Hohenschwangau emporragt. Sonst ist diese immerhin 1,9 km lange und 62 m tiefe Wasserfläche ganz zwischen dunkle Waldhänge und Höhenzüge gebettet, ein ungewöhnliches Bild für einen See im Ostallgäu. Stets am Ufer entlang führt ein Rundwanderweg. An heißen Sommertagen schwimmen auch einige Mutige in diesem stets kühlen Bergwasser.

Only at the easternmost corner of the Alpsee are there a few buildings, Hohenschwangau Castle towering up in close proximity above them. Otherwise the lake, 1.9 km long and 62m deep, is surrounded by dark forests and mountain ridges, an unusual sight in the East Allgäu. A trail follows the shore all the way round, and there are some more peaceful alternatives higher up the slopes. On hot summer days a few hardy souls brave the cold mountain water.

Solo nell'angolo orientale del lago si trovano delle case, ma sopra di esse sorge il castello Hohenschwangau. Il lago, che è lungo 1,9 chilometri e profondo 62 m giace tra foreste e colline, un'immagine insolita per l'Algovia orientale. Molto bello è il lungofiume e più in alto ci sono cammini molto pacifici e belli. In estate quando fa caldo alcune persone coraggiose si tuffano nell'acqua gelida del lago alpino.

## SCHLOSS HOHENSCHWANGAU, Südansicht / View from the south / Veduta da sud

Hohenschwangau heißt der Ort am Fuß der berühmten Königsschlösser; Schwan- und Alpsee liegen in seiner Nähe. In beiden spiegelt sich das Schloß mit dem gleichlautenden Namen, in dem Ludwig II. Jahre seiner Jugend verbracht hat. Die Wandgemälde des Schlosses über die Themen der Deutschen Mythologie, regten ihn später zu einer ähnlichen Ausgestaltung von Neuschwanstein an. Die 1837 vollendete Anlage steht beherrschend auf einem 864 m hohen Bergrücken. Der Palas mit seinen vier Türmen gibt dem Schloß seine unverwechselbare Note.

Hohenschwangau is the name of the village nestling beneath the royal castles; Swan Lake and the Alpsee are close by. Both reflect the image of the castle of the same name where Ludwig II spent his youth. The paintings on the castle walls depicting scenes from German mythology, inspired him to create similar decorations in Neuschwanstein. The complex, completed in 1837, rises up in its dominating position on a 864 metre-high mountain ridge. The main living quarters with the four towers give the castle its own unmistakable stamp.

Si chiama Hohenschwangau il paese ai piedi dei famosi castelli reali. Molto vicini sono i due laghi Schwansee e Alpsee. In tutti e due i laghi si rispecchia il castello nel quale Ludovico II ha trascorso la sua giovinezza. Le pitture murali all'interno del castello mostrando scene della mitologia tedesca lo ispiravano all'allestimento simile del castello Neuschwanstein. Il castello fu finito nel 1837 ed è situato su una colline di 864 m di altezza. Il palazzo con le sue quattro torri da l'inconfondibile caratteristica al castello.

## FÜSSEN am Lech

Das Foto zeigt alle wichtigen Teile Füssens, den Lech, das ehemalige Kloster, die reizvolle Barockkirche St. Mang, das steil über den Häusern aufragende Hohe Schloß, welches ehemals Bischofssitz war, und die eng verschachtelte Altstadt, die heute Fußgängerzone ist und zu einem gemütlichen Bummel einlädt. Schon die Römer hatten an dieser Stelle, wo ihre Via Claudia Augusta aus den Bergen kommend das Vorland erreichte, ein Kastell errichtet, das sie Foetibus nannten. Heute bildet Füssen das Zentrum einer der beliebtesten Ferienregionen.

The photo shows all the most important parts of Füssen, the Lech, the former monastery, the charming baroque church of St. Mang, the High Castle and former bishop's residence rising up steeply above the houses, and the intricate network of streets in the old town, now a pedestrian precinct, all inviting the visitor to take a quiet stroll. As long ago as Roman times a camp and fort were established here where the Via Claudia Augusta enters the foreland. It was called Foetibus. Today Füssen is the centre of one of the most popular holiday areas.

La foto mostra tutte le parti importanti di Füssen, il fiume Lech, il vecchio convento, la graziosa chiesa barocca di St. Mang, il castello Hohes Schloß, situato in alto che fu sede del vescovo e il centro storico, oggi zona pedonale che invita ad andare a passeggio. Già i romani avevano costruito qui, dove arriva la Via Claudia Augusta dalle Alpi, un castello chiamato Foetibus. Oggi Füssen è uno dei centri turistici più importanti di tutta la regione.

## WEISSENSEE mit Blick zum Säuling

Ostallgäuer Bilderbuch-Landschaft: der Weißensee schmiegt sich an steile, bewaldete Berghänge, und in seiner weiten Wasserfläche spiegelt sich der 2047 m hohe Säuling, der auffallendste Berg der Region. Auf den Höhen in der Nähe thronen die Burgruinen von Hohenfreyberg und Eisenberg, und schon auf einem richtigen Gipfel stehen die Reste des Falkensteins (1267 m). Dort oben wollte König Ludwig II. ein noch mächtigeres Schloß als Neuschwanstein errichten; doch mehr als ein Modell kam nicht zustande.

East Allgäu picturebook landscape: the Weissensee nestling against steep, wooded slopes, and the 2047 metre-high Säuling, the most prominent mountain in the region, reflected in its waters. On the heights nearby, the towering castle ruins of the Hohenfreyberg and Eisenberg, and the remains of the Falkenstein (1267 m) right up on a summit. This is where King Ludwig wanted to build another castle, even mightier than Neuschwanstein; but the project never got past the completion of a model.

Un paesaggio favoloso dell'Algovia orientale: Il lago Weißensee giace nel mezzo di colline con foreste e nella sua vasta superficie si specchia il monte Säuling (2047 m), la montagna più imponente della regione. Sulle colline attorno si trovano le rovine Hohenfreyberg e Eisenberg e in cima di una piccola montagna troviamo le rovine del Falkenstein (1267 m). Lì il re Ludovico II voleva costruire un castello ancora più magnifico di Neuschwanstein, ma non si è passato oltre il modello.

# PFRONTEN / Ostallgäu, Ortsteil Berg

Pfronten füllt ein weites, sonniges Tal, das im Norden von einigen Hügeln begrenzt wird, während es im Süden mächtige Berge einschließen, unter denen der 1987 m hohe Aggenstein dominiert. Dieses Ferien-Dorado besteht aus 13 einst selbstständigen Dörfern, die heute stark zusammengewachsen sind. Ein besonderes Kuriosum: hier fließen die Bäche, etwa die Faule Ache, nicht nach Norden, sondern in die Berge hinein; so bildet Steinach, der südlichste Ortsteil Pfrontens, mit 850 m den tiefsten Bereich des Gemeindegebietes.

Pfronten fills a broad, sunny valley, closed off to the north by a few hills, but to the south by mighty mountains, predominant among them the 1987 metre-high Aggenstein. This holiday-maker's paradise is made up of 13 formerly individual villages, which today have grown very close together. One particular oddity: the streams here, for example the Faule Ache, don't flow north, but towards the mountains. Steinach, the southernmost part of Pfronten at an altitude of 850 m, is the lowest in the whole community.

Pfronten è situato in una larga e soleggiata valle, limitata a nord da alcune colline e a sud da imponenti massicci alpini, come per esempio l'Aggenstein (1987 m). Questo centro turistico comprende 13 paesi autonomi che oggi però sono diventati un insieme. Una curiosità del posto, i ruscelli come la Faule Ache non vanno verso nord, ma verso le Alpi. Il quartiere Steinach con una altezza di 850 m è il quartiere più basso di tutto il comune.

## PFRONTEN / Ostallgäu, Trachtenfest / Folk costume festival / Feste popolari

Spazierengehen, wandern, bergsteigen sind die liebsten Beschäftigungen der Gäste in Pfronten und ähnlichen Orten. Zur Abwechslung und bei schlechtem Wetter bewundert man vielleicht eine der vielen Dorfkirchen, die meist liebevoll barock ausgestaltet sind, wie die 1696 fertig gestellte Pfarrkirche St. Nikolaus in Pfronten-Berg, die malerisch auf einer Anhöhe liegt. Ihr Turmdach stellt eine umgestülpte Enzianblüte dar. Trachtenumzüge oder -feste locken zusätzlich Einheimische und Fremde an.

Walking, hiking, mountain climbing - these are the most popular pastimes of visitors to Pfronten and other places like it. For a change or when the weather is poor, they may go and see one of the many village churches, usually lovingly decorated in baroque style, such as the parish church of St. Nicholas in Pfronten-Berg, completed in 1696 and picturesquely situated on a rise. The roof on the tower has the shape of an upturned gentian flower. Folk costume parades and festivals draw visitors and locals alike.

Paseggiare, camminare nelle colline e praticare l'alpinismo ecco le attività preferite degli ospiti di Pfronten e intorni. Quando fa brutto tempo si possono ammirare le tante chiese parrocchiali tutte allestite in stile barocco come la chiesa St. Nikolaus a Pfronten-Berg, finita nel 1696 situata su un'idillica collina. Il suo tetto rappresenta un fiore di genziana capovolto. In più anche sfilate folcloristiche e feste popolari attraggono sia gli abitanti che visitatori da fuori.

# NESSELWANG / Ostallgäu, Pfarrkirche St. Andreas / Parish church St. Andrew / Chiesa St. Andreas

Das in ein kleines Tal geschmiegte Nesselwang zählt zu den typischen Orten des Alpenrandes. Im Süden steigen die meist bewaldeten Hänge steil zu den ersten Gipfeln empor; der Edelsberg ist bereits 1629 m hoch. Richtung Nordosten hingegen zieht sich das Ostallgäuer Voralpenland hin. Freie Wiesenflächen, Moore, verträumte Seen, Bergkuppen und Wälder sorgen für eine Region voller Abwechslung. Es ist ein auffallend stilles Land mit einzelnen Höfen und Weilern, obwohl es so nahe an den lebhaften Ferienorten liegt.

Nesselwang nestling in a small valley is typical of many places on the edge of the Alps. To the south the mostly wooded slopes rise steeply to the first range of mountains; the Edelsberg is already 1629 m high. But to the northeast the countryside stretches out as it does everywhere in the foothills of the East Allgäu. Open meadowland, moor, little lakes, rounded hilltops and forest create a landscape full of variety. It is a remarkably peaceful stretch of countryside with solitary farmsteads and hamlets, despite its proximity to the busy holiday resorts.

Nesselwang è situato in una piccola valle ed è uno dei paesi tipici della regione. A sud il paesaggio è dominato da colline boscose che arrivano a un'altezza notevole come l'Edelsberg con 1629 m. A nord-est invece vediamo l'altopiano dell'Algovia orientale. Ampi prati, paludi, laghetti incantati, colline, boschi offrono all'ospite un paesaggio molto svariato. E una regione molto silenziosa e pacifica con singole fattorie e paesini nonostante la vicinanza con i centri turistici.

## GRÜNTENSEE, Stausee der Wertach

Nördlich des Wintersport- und Ferienortes Oberjoch entspringt die Wertach. Sie ist anfangs ein eher unscheinbarer Berg- und Wiesenbach, der jedoch später als zentraler Fluß in der Großstadt Augsburg „Karriere" macht. Bevor die Wertach bei Nesselwang in einer sehr langen, einsamen Waldschlucht verschwindet, wird sie zum 2,4 km langen Grüntensee aufgestaut, der zwischen sanften, freundlichen Wiesen liegt. Weit im Hintergrund ragt der namensgebende Grünten (1738 m) auf, ein bekannter Aussichtsberg.

North of the wintersport and holiday resort of Oberjoch is the source of the Wertach. To begin with, it is a rather inconspicuous little mountain stream flowing through the fields, later, however, it will really make it to the top as the river of the great city of Augsburg. Before the Wertach disappears into a long, lonely, wooded gorge near Nesselwang, it is dammed up to create the 2.4 km-long Grüntensee, lying in the midst of gentle, soft meadowlands. Far away in the background the mountain that gives it its name towers up 1738 m high, a peak popular for its fine view.

A nord del centro turistico alpino Oberjoch nasce il fiume Wertach. All'inizio si presenta come un ruscello qualsiasi ma più avanti diventa fiume centrale della grande città di Augsburg. Prima che la Wertach sparisca vicino a Nesselwang in una gola stretta in mezzo ai boschi, viene sbarrata nella diga Grüntensee con una lunghezza di 2,4 km. La diga si trova in mezzo a prati bellissimi e nel fondo domina il monte Grünten (1783 m) che ha dato il nome alla diga e che dall'alto da delle vedute meravigliose.

Schon mitten in den Bergen, im weiten Becken des Illertals, liegt Sonthofen, das Zentrum des Oberallgäus und die südlichste Stadt Deutschlands. Alle malerischen Plätze, mit denen die Region so reich gesegnet ist, lassen sich von hier aus schnell erreichen, etwa die Starzlachklamm mit ihren senkrechten Wänden oder der so ins Auge fallende Aussichtsberg Grünten (1738 m). Von dessen Gipfel schaut man wie aus dem Flugzeug auch auf die Niedersonthofener Seen, ein Dorado für Badenixen wie Fotofreunde.

Sonthofen, the centre of the Upper Allgäu and the southernmost town in Germany, is already up in the midst of the mountains, in a broad basin of the Iller valley. All the many scenic places in the region are easily accessible from here, for example the Starzlachklamm with its vertical rockfaces or the eye-catching Grünten (1738m) with its fine view. From the summit you have an aerial view, as if from high up in a plane, down to the Niedersonthofen lakes, an Eldorado for bathing beauties and photographers.

Sonthofen si trova già in mezzo alle Alpi in un bacino della Iller. E il centro dell'Algovia alta e la città più meridionale delle Germania. Tutti i posti incantevoli si possono raggiungere in poco tempo, come la Sterzachklamm con le sue pareti verticali e il monte panoramico Grünten (1738 m). Dalla sua cima si ha una veduta come dall'aereo sui laghi die Niedersonthofen, un vero paradiso per gli amanti del bagno e della fotografia.

## HINDELANG / OBERSTDORF / OBERSTDORF und Rubihorn

Bei Sonthofen zweigt aus dem Tal der Iller das Ostrachtal ab, in dem, sich am sanften Sonnenhang empor ziehend, der Markt Hindelang liegt, ein Ferienort und zugleich das Tor zu den großen Gipfeln um den Hochvogel (2592 m). Ganz im Süden des Oberallgäus aber füllt Oberstdorf (815 m) den großzügigen Bergkessel, ein berühmter Name, der jährlich Tausende von Gästen anzieht. Alles wird hier geboten: Hotels der Upperclass, Kaffeehäuser, urige Gasthöfe, Wanderwege, Sprungschanzen, Loipen, Pisten, Wildwasser, Berge, Natur ohne Ende ...

The market-town of Hindelang stretches out up the gentle, sun-soaked slope of the Ostrach valley, which branches off the Iller valley near Sonthofen. Hindelang is a holiday resort and the gateway to the high peaks around the Hochvogel (2592m). In the very south of the Upper Allgäu, Oberstdorf (815m) fills the basin amidst the mountains, a famous name which draws thousands of visitors. All needs are catered for: top-class hotels, cafes, old-fashioned inns, hiking trails, ski-jumps, cross-country loipes, downhill pistes, mountain torrents, mountains, nature in abundance ...

Vicino a Sonthofen si incontrano due valli, quelli della Iller e l'Ostrachtal nel quale si trova il paese Hindelang, situato su una collina molto soleggiata. Hindelang è sia un centro turistico che la porta alle montagne alte dell'Algovia come il Hochvogel (2592 m). Ma nell'estremo sud si trova Oberstdorf (815 m), un centro famoso che ogni anno attira migliaia di ospiti. Oberstdorf offre di tutto: alberghi lussuosi, caffè, osterie locali tipiche, cammini per i boschi, trampolini di salto alpino, piste per lo sci di fondo, piste per lo sci alpino, torrenti, montagne, una natura infinita ....

## OBERSTDORF, Skigebiet auf der Fellhorn Höhe (1967 m)

Sieben Täler münden bei Oberstdorf ins Illertal. Jedes mit eigenem Charakter und unverwechselbarem Charme. Das zerklüftete Trettachtal etwa mit seiner imposanten Bergwelt, das wilde Oytal oder das sanfte Stillachtal, mittendrin aber findet sich Oberstdorf in einem der sonnenreichsten Gebiete Bayerns. Oberstdorf, südlichster Kur- und Erholungsort Deutschlands. Zusammen mit dem benachbarten Kleinwalsertal ist Oberstdorf das größte Wander-, Berg- und Skisportgebiet am Nordrand der Alpen.

Seven valleys converge near Oberstdorf, joining the Iller valley. Each has its own character and unmistakable charm. The clefted Trettach valley, for example, with its imposing mountain scenery, the wild Oy valley or the gentle Stillach valley. In their midst is Oberstdorf in one of the sunniest regions of the whole of Bavaria. Oberstdorf is the southernmost spa resort in Germany. It is the centre of a hiking, mountaineering and skiing region that takes in the adjacent Kleinwalsertal, the largest such area on the northern edge of the Alps.

Sette valli si congiungono nella Illertal, all'altezza di Oberstdorf, ognuna con il suo proprio carattere e fascino inconfondibili. La frastagliata Trettachtal con le sue imponenti cime, la selvaggia Oytal o la dolce Stillachtal, abbracciano Oberstdorf in una delle regioni più assolate della Baviera. Oberstdorf è il luogo termale e di cura più a sud della Germania. Assieme alla vicina Kleinwalsertal, Oberstdorf è a nord delle Alpi la regione più grande di sport invernali e turismo alpestre.

## OBERSTDORF

Ein Muss für den Oberstdorfbesucher ist ein Ausflug, egal ob mit dem Stellwagen, Pferdeschlitten, den Langlaufski oder zu Fuß in eines der Oberstdorfer Täler. Berühmt ist Oberstdorf auch wegen der umfangreichen Sprungschanzenanlagen, wo alljährlich weltbekannte Wettkämpfe ausgetragen werden. Neben vieler Sehenswürdigkeiten, sowie sportlichen Aktivitäten und Traditionsfesten kommt die Gemütlichkeit nicht zu kurz und dann hat die Winterzeit ihren ganz besonderen Reiz.

## OBERSTDORF

An absolute must for any visitor to Oberstdorf is an excursion into one of the Oberstdorf valleys by horse-drawn wagon or sleigh, or on foot. Oberstdorf is also known for its ski-jumping facilities, where world-famous competitions are held every year. Alongside the bustle of the sights, sports events and traditional festivals, German "Gemütlichkeit" thrives, and then wintertime has its own very special charm.

## OBERSTDORF

Per il visitatore a Oberstdorf, è obbligatorio compiere una gita in una delle valli circostanti, sia essa con la diligenza, con la slitta a cavalli, gli sci da fondo o a piedi. Oberstdorf è famosa anche per i numerosi trampolini da sci, dove durante tutto l'anno si svolgono competizioni note in tutto il mondo. Oltre alle numerose curiosità, alle attività sportive e alle feste tradizionali, la comodità non viene trascurata e qui la stagione invernale offre il suo fascino particolare.

Früher benötigte man einen ganzen Tag um einen Alpengipfel zu erreichen. Heute braucht man dazu nur noch Minuten, denn die Bergbahnen sind wahre Gipfelstürmer. Oben angekommen, ob auf den Pfaden des Wandersmannes oder mit der Bergbahn kann man Atem schöpfen, Kraft tanken, Tiere wie Gämsen und Murmeltiere beobachten. Im Winter ist das Skifahren angesagt aber im Sommer geht man auf Entdeckungsreise über Stock und Stein. Man kann die Berge erklimmen und Flora und Fauna der Hochbergwelt erkunden.

In the past you needed a whole day to reach the summit of one of the mountains. Today it's often just a matter of minutes, as the cable cars race you to the top. When you've reached the summit, whether by hiking trail or cableway, you can breathe in the pure mountain air, recharge your batteries and observe wildlife, including chamois and marmots. In winter, the agenda is skiing, but in the summer you can take off on a voyage of discovery, up hill and down dale, through the flora and fauna of the mountain scenery. The Fellhorn is otherwise known, and

Nel passato, era necessario un giorno intero per raggiungere una vetta alpina. Oggi bastano appena alcuni minuti, poiché le ferrovie di montagna sono vere scalatrici. Arrivati in cima, lungo il percorso dei viandanti o con la ferrovia, si fa una sosta, si ritemprano le forze, si osservano gli stambecchi e le marmotte - dove meglio che in montagna? D'inverno è d'obbligo sciare, ma d'estate si va alla ventura. Ci si arrampica sulle montagne e si scoprono la flora e la fauna delle sommità alpine. Il Fellhorn è chiamato propriamente anche Montagna dei Fiori perché qui

# ALLGÄU ALPINE PANORAMA / Panorama alpestre dell'ALLGÄU

Das „Fellhorn" trägt völlig zu Recht den Beinamen „der Blumenberg". Hier wachsen in großer Zahl seltene Pflanzen und Blumen vom Frühjahr bis in den Herbst. Höhepunkt der farbenfrohen Pracht ist die Alpenrosenblüte, die den Berg im Juni und Juli mit einem leuchtend roten Blütenmeer überzieht. Beim Abstieg schaut man auf das Panorama der Allgäuer Almen - auch „Alpen" genannt, welche bereits seit 1000 Jahren genutzt werden. Die schonende Beweidung der Almen hilft mit die Bildung von Lawinen und Erosionen zu vermeiden.

rightly so, as Flower Mountain. Its slopes are covered with a profusion of flowers and plants, some of them rare, from springtime through to the autumn. The climax is the colourful blossoming of the Alpine roses, covering the mountain with a sea of bright red bloom in June and July. On the way back down you can see the Alps – the Allgäu term for the alpine pastures that have existed for over a thousand years. Careful, controlled grazing helps to prevent avalanches and erosion.

crescono innumerevoli piante e fiori dalla primavera all'autunno. Il culmine di questa magnificenza di colori è la fioritura dei rododendri, che ricoprono la montagna in giugno e luglio con un mare scintillante di fiori rossi. Nella discesa si vedono i pascoli - gli abitanti del luogo li chiamano Alpi - che esistono da almeno 1000 anni. Il manto erboso dei pascoli aiuta a prevenire la formazione di valanghe e di erosioni.

## EINÖDSBACH mit Trettachspitze (2595m) — NEBELHORN mit dem Seealpsee und den Höfrats im Hintergrund

In Einödsbach stehen die südlichsten Häuser Deutschlands. Auf einer Geländestufe hoch über dem Flüßchen Stillach findet man diesen Weiler mit seiner imposanten Bergkulisse, in der die Trettachspitze (2595 m) dominiert. Viele Neugierige zieht dieser malerische Bergwinkel an. Stiller ist es oben am Seealpsee, den man nach einer Wanderung von etwa 40 Minuten von der Nebelhornbahn aus erreicht. Anschließend steigt mancher von dort auf steinigem Pfad ins Oytal hinab und wandert nach Oberstdorf zurück.

Einödsbach is where the southernmost houses in Germany are to be found. This mountain hamlet is situated on a plateau up above the river Stillach, amidst impressive mountain scenery dominated by the Trettachspitze (2595m). This picturesque little corner of Germany is a popular place to visit. If you're looking for something more peaceful, try the Seealpsee, about a forty-minute hike from the Nebelhorn cablecar station. If you like, you can carry on from there along the stony footpath that takes you down into the Oy valley and back to Oberstdorf.

A Einödsbach si trovano le case più meridionali di tutta la Germania. Su uno scalino sul fiumicello Stillach si trova questo paesino davanti a un fondo imponente di montagne dominato dal monte Trettachspitze (2995 m). Vengono sempre molti ospiti curiosi per vedere quest'angolo pittoresco. Ancora più pacifico è il paesaggio attorno al lago Seealpsee che si raggiunge in circa 40 minuti a piedi partendo dalla funivia del monte Nebelhorn. Da lì si può scendere a piedi su cammini alpini all'Oytal per tornare poi a Oberstdorf.

## ALLGÄUER ALPEN, Nebelhorn mit Blick auf die Gipfelstation der Nebelhornbahn / cableway station / stazione di arrivo della teleferica

Rund 15 Millionen Menschen hat sie auf das 2224 Meter hohe Nebelhorn befördert und dabei eine Strecke von 54 Erdumrundungen oder dreimal zum Mond und zurück absolviert: Die Nebelhornbahn, einst die längste Personenseilschwebebahn der Welt, maßgeblicher Motor der touristischen Entwicklung Oberstdorfs und die höchste Seilbahn im Allgäu. Sie wurde bereits am 10.06.1930 in Betrieb genommen. Nebelhorn und Fellhorn bieten ein umfangreiches Freizeitangebot, welches sich mit der Umwelt gut vereinbaren lässt.

The cable cars of the Nebelhornbahn have transported about 15 million people up to the top of the 2224m-high Nebelhorn, covering a distance corresponding to 54 times the earth's circumference or three times to the moon and back. It is one of the longest cableways in the world, the highest in the Allgäu, a magnet drawing visitors from far and wide to Oberstdorf, promoting and sustaining the growth of tourism in the area. It was taken into service on 10th June 1930. The Nebelhorn and Fellhorn offer a wide range of environment-friendly leisure-time activities.

Circa 15 milioni di persone ha portato sulla cima del Nebelhorn, a 2224 metri sul mare, e così compiuto 54 giri attorno al mondo oppure tre viaggi sulla luna andata e ritorno: la teleferica del Nebelhorn, una delle più lunghe del mondo, motore decisivo dello sviluppo turistico di Oberstdorf e la più alta teleferica dell'Allgäu, entrò in servizio il 10.06.1930. Il Nebelhorn e il Fellhorn offrono ogni tipo di attività per il tempo libero, che si armonizzano bene con l'ambiente.

## KLEINWALSERTAL, Mittelberg-Walmerdingerhorn

Das Kleinwalsertal umfasst die drei Ortschaften Hirschegg, Riezlern und Mittelberg. In dieser eindrucksvollen Karstlandschaft findet man viele Höhlen und eine artenreiche Pflanzen- und Tierwelt, Wasserfälle, Strudellöcher und Naturbrücken sowie zahlreiche Moorbiotope. Bei einem Spaziergang durch das Kleinwalsertal können Sie noch eine ganze Anzahl sehr alte Walserhäuser finden. Mit ihren sonnenverbrannten Fassaden erinnern sie an die Zeit, in der das Kleinwalsertal noch eine Streusiedlung und reines Bergbauerngebiet war.

The Kleinwalsertal comprises the three villages of Hirschegg, Riezlern and Mittelberg. It is set in impressive scenery that includes a large number of caves, a multitude of species of flora and fauna, waterfalls, natural whirlpools and bridges, as well as numerous moorland biotopes. On a walk through the Kleinwalsertal you will still see a considerable number of very old local buildings. Their sunburnt facades are a reminder of the time when the valley was sparsely settled, home only to the mountain farmers.

La Kleinwalsertal è una valle che racchiude le tre località Hirschegg, Riezlern e Mittelberg. In questo impressionante paesaggio carsico si trovano molte caverne e una ricca fauna e flora, cascate, voragini e ponti naturali, così come molti biotopi palustri. Con una passeggiata lungo la Kleinwalsertal si può scoprire tutta una serie di antiche case valligiane. Con le loro facciate bruciate dal sole esse ricordano i tempi in cui la Kleinwalsertal era esclusivamente terra di minatori che dormivano su letti di paglia.

## HEILBRONNER WEG / Allgäuer Alpen / Allgäu mountains / Alpi dell´Algovia

Im Herzen der Allgäuer Alpen liegen zwei der größten Hütten des Alpenvereins, die Kemptner und die Rappenseehütte. Der Heilbronner Weg verbindet diese Stützpunkte. Doch darf bei dem Wort „Weg" niemand eine bequeme Promenade für jedermann erwarten. Diese berühmte Route führt teilweise durch richtiges Felsgelände. Im Gestein verankerte Drahtseile, Leitern usw. ermöglichen auch einem Bergwanderer, der allerdings alpine Erfahrung braucht, diesen einmaligen Gang über den bis 2615 m hohen Grat.

In the heart of the Allgäu Alps are two of the largest mountain lodges maintained by the Alpine Association, the Kemptner and the Rappensee lodge. The Heilbronner Path connects the two. But don't be misled to assume the word "path" means an easy walk. In some places this famous route is very rocky. Only the iron ropes, ladders etc. anchored in the rocks make the spectacular trail along the up to 2615 metre-high ridge passable, and then only for those with Alpine experience.

Nel cuore delle Alpi dell'Algovia si trovano i due rifugi alpini più grandi dell'associazione alpinistica, i rifugi Kemptner Hütte e Rappenseehütte. Il cammino alpino Heilbronner Weg collega i due rifugi. Ma la parola "cammino" non significa certamente un sentiero commodo per tutti, ma questa rotta famosa va attraverso un paesaggio montuoso. Ma tramite funi di accaio, scale ecc. l'alpinista esperto riesce a fare questo magnifico cammino sulle cime in una altezza di 2615 m.

## ENZIAN-BERGWIESE

◁ **OYTAL, Blick auf den Schneck**

Von Oberstdorf zieht das Oytal, in dem ein Gasthaus liegt, zwischen die großen Berge hinein. Dort fasziniert dann der Blick auf den Schneck (2268 m), einen aus Fels und steilstem Grat aufgebauten Berg, der im weißen „Wintermantel" besonders imposant aussieht.

◁ **OY VALLEY, View to the Schneck**

The Oy valley, which starts in Oberstdorf and has an inn, lies between high mountains on either side. It offers a fascinating view of the Schneck (2268m), a steep, both rocky and ridge-clad mountain that looks especially impressive in its "winter coat".

◁ **OYTAL, Veduta sul monte Schneck**

Da Oberstdorf parte la valle Oytal dove si trova un'osteria tipica. E affascinante la veduta sul monte Schneck (2268 m), formato da rocce e cereste ripide che d'inverno quando è coperto di neve offre una vista bellissimo.

**ZIPFELSBACHFÄLLE** ▷

Immer mehr Wanderer entdecken den besonderen Reiz des winterlich verschneiten und vereisten Hochgebirges. Manches kleinere Ziel, wie Berggasthäuser oder die Zipfelsbachfälle bei Hinterstein, läßt sich auch in der kalten Jahreszeit von jedermann erreichen.

**ZIPFELSBACH WATERFALLS** ▷

More and more hikers are discovering the special appeal of the mountains in winter's ice and snow. There are many places such as mountain inns or the Zipfelbach falls near Hinterstein that are easy enough for anyone to reach, even in the winter months.

**ZIPFELSBACHFÄLLE** ▷

Sempre più ospiti amanti dell'alpinismo scoprono il fascino della montagna durante l'inverno quando tutto è coperto di neve e ghiaccio. Ci sono alcune mete come osterie alpine o le cascate Zipfelsbachfälle vicino a Hinterstein che sono accessibili per tutti in ogni stagione.

## RAPPENSEE / Allgäuer Alpen, Sonnenuntergang / Sunset / Tramonto

Nicht nur im Alpenvorland schmücken zahllose Seen das Allgäu. Auch hoch oben in den Bergen versteckt sich manche, oft tiefblaue Wasserfläche, in der sich wilde Felsgipfel spiegeln. Durch zahlreiche außergewöhnliche Aufnahmen wurde der Rappensee berühmt. Ganz in der Nähe liegt nämlich die gleichnamige Hütte. So läßt sich hier ideal ein Sonnenuntergang fotografieren. An keinem anderen See über 2000 m Höhe ist sonst ein Mensch zu dieser Tageszeit unterwegs!

It is not only in the foothills that the countryside is decorated with numerous lakes. High up in the mountains too there is many a hidden, deep-blue tarn in which the craggy peaks are reflected. The Rappensee became well-known for the countless stunning photos taken there. Very close by is the Alpine refuge of the same name, making it an ideal place to photograph sunsets. Elsewhere not a soul is to be found by a lake at this altitude at this time of day.

Non soltanto nell'altopiano delle Alpi si trovano numerosi laghi, ma anche qui in mezzo alle montagne si nascondono tanti laghi nelle quali si specchiano le cime delle montagne alte. Tramite delle foto straordinarie il Rappensee è diventato famoso. Vicino al lago si trova un rifugio con lo stesso nome. Un posto ideale per fotografare i tramonti. In nessun altro posto si vede a quest'ora una persona in 2000 m di altezza!

## BREITACHKLAMM

Die Breitach, einer der drei Iller-Quellflüsse, hat sich in unermüdlicher Kleinarbeit einen Weg durch sehr harte Felsen „gefräst". So entstand die berühmte Breitachklamm westlich von Oberstdorf, die 1500 m lang ist und sich bis zu 100 m tief einschneidet. Die oft muschelförmig ausgewaschenen Wände sind meist senkrecht und stehen manchmal nur wenige Meter auseinander. Schon 1905 baute man den ersten Steig durch die Schlucht. Ein Ausflug in diese Felsenwelt ist noch heute für jeden ein Erlebnis.

## BREITACH GORGE

The Breitach, one of the three tributaries of the Iller, has eaten its way, millimetre by millimetre in tireless labour, through the hard rocks, thus creating the famous Breitach gorge west of Oberstdorf. It is 1500m long and up to 100m deep. The rockfaces, washed out by the water into shell-shaped curves, are mostly vertical and only a few metres apart. The first path through the gorge was built as long ago as 1905. A trip to this rockworld is an experience not to be missed.

## BREITACHKLAMM

Il fiume Breitach, uno dei tre fiumi sorgenti della Iller si è creato in millioni di anni un cammino attraverso rocce molto dure. Così si formò la famosa Breitachklamm ad ovest di Oberstdorf con una lunghezza di 1500 m e una profondità di 100 m. Le rocce lavate sono verticali e spesso divise da una distanza di pochi metri. Già nel 1905 si è costruito il prima cammino attraverso la gola. Un'escursione in questo mondo sotto terra è un momento impressionante per tutti ancora oggi.

## 42 GUNZESRIED, Blick auf Alpe Egg und Daumen / View towards Alpe Egg and Daumen / Veduta su Alpe Egg e Daumen

Je weiter man nach Süden kommt, desto mächtiger ragen die Gipfel der Allgäuer Alpen auf, eines der größten und höchsten Gebirge Deutschlands. Bei Gunzesried in einem Nebental des Oberallgäus bestimmen Wiesen und Alpweiden, auf denen das Vieh den Sommer verbringt, noch stark das Landschaftsbild. Der Bergwanderer findet hier ein Dorado für seine Unternehmungen; er steigt vielleicht zu den Alphütten hinauf oder gar auf die Gipfel, die trotz des oft felsigen Geländes alle mit Steigen erschlossen sind.

The further south you go, the more mighty the peaks of the Allgäu mountains become. Near Gunzesried in a side valley of the Upper Allgäu, the meadows and pastures where the cattle spend the summer still characterise the landscape. This is an Eldorado for mountain-hiking: you can climb up to the Alpine huts or the summits, all of which in fact, despite the rocky terrain, are accessible on established footpaths.

Più si va verso sud più alte diventano le montagne delle Alpi dell'Algovia, una delle catene montuose più grandi ed alte della Germania. Vicino a Gunzesried in una valle secondaria dell'Algovia alta il paesaggio è ancora dominato da prati e pascoli alpini, dove d'estate pascola il bestiame. Chi ama l'alpinismo trova qui un eldorado per le sue escursioni, può salire fino ai pascoli alpini e perfino sulle cime che si possono raggiungere con l'aiuto di scale alpine.

### OSTERTALTOBEL im Gunzesried

In allen Teilen der Allgäuer Alpen gehören die felsigen Schluchten, hier Tobel genannt, Klammen und Wasserfälle, zu den reizvollsten Ausflugszielen. Erstaunlicherweise sind nur Breitach- und Starzlachklamm allgemein bekannt, obwohl zu etwa zwanzig anderen „Wasserspielen" gute Pfade führen. Dazu zählt auch der Ostertaltobel auf dem Foto, den man in wenigen Minuten von Gunzesried-Säge aus erreicht. Er bietet malerisch mit Moos überzogenes Blockwerk, kulissenartige Felsrippen und fünf kleine Wasserfälle.

### OSTERTALTOBEL at Gunzesried

All over the Allgäu the rocky gorges (called "Tobel"), ravines and waterfalls are among the most attractive destinations for a day out. Rather surprisingly, only the Breitach and Starzlach gorges are well-known, although there are well-marked paths leading to about twenty other "waterworks", Including, for example, the Ostertaltobel in the photo, which is just a few minutes from Gunzesried-Säge. There you will find boulders picturesquely covered in moss, rockfaces like theatre backdrops, and five small waterfalls.

### OSTERTALTOBEL nel Gunzesried

In tutte le parti delle Alpi dell'Algovia le gole rocciose, chiamate "Tobel", fanno parte del paesaggio. Normalmente si conosce sole le gole Breitachklamm e Starzlachklamm, anche se ci sono cammini ben curati fino a venti altre gole. Tra essi c'è anche l'Ostertaltobel sulla foto che si raggiunge in pochi minuti da Gunzesried-Säge. Offre al visitatore impressionanti formazioni rocciose ricoperte di musco e cinque piccole cascate.

## OBERSTAUFEN, Ferien- und Schrothkurort / Spa / Centro turistico e di cure

Wer von Immenstadt am Alpsee vorbei Richtung Westen fährt, kommt bald nach Oberstaufen (791 m), dem die Schrothkuren zu einem berühmten Namen verhalfen. Hier empfängt den Besucher das Flair eines echten Kurortes mit schicken Geschäften, Kaffeehäusern und Ausflugsgaststätten. Das reizvolle Umland, eine stark gegliederte Landschaft mit viel freien Wiesen, versteckten Dörfern, aussichtsreichen Höhen, den eindrucksvollen Buchenegger Wasserfällen, den großen Bergen im Hintergrund verlockt zu kleinen und großen Exkursionen.

Leaving Immenstadt westwards, past the Alpsee, you soon reach Oberstaufen (791m), which achieved fame through its Schroth's treatments. Visitors are caught up in the flair of a real spa with smart shops, cafes and restaurants. The charming countryside round about: broad meadowlands, tucked-away villages, hilltops with fine views, the impressive Buchenegger waterfalls. The high mountains in the background are a temptation to embark on short or more extensive excursions.

Partendo da Immenstadt verso ovest si arriva presto a Oberstaufen (791 m) famosa per le cure disidratanti di Schroth. L'atmosfera accogliente del paese con i suoi negozi, caffè e ristoranti affascina ogni ospite. Il paesaggio incantevole con molti ampi prati, paesini nascosti, colline panoramiche e le impressionanti cascate di Buchenegger e le alte montagne nel fondo incuriosiscono il visitatore ad esplorare la regione.

## VIEHSCHEID, Almabtrieb

Auf knapp 600 Alpen, wie die Almen im Allgäu stets genannt werden, verbringen etwa 30 000 Stück Vieh den Sommer. Gab es keine Unfälle, schmückt man im späten September die Kühe und treibt sie, begleitet vom Dröhnen der Kuhglocken, ins Tal zum Scheideplatz, wo die Herden wieder aufgeteilt, „geschieden«, werden. In vielen Orten wie Oberstdorf, Hindelang, Gunzesried entwickelte sich der Almabtrieb, hier als Viehscheid bekannt, zu einem Volksfest mit Bierzelten und vielen Gästen.

## DRIVING CATTLE DOWN

There are about 600 Alpine pastures in the Allgäu where some 30,000 cattle spend the summer. If the summer was accident-free, the cows are dekked out in late September and, to the resounding of their bells, driven down to the "Scheidplatz" where the herds are split up again, each to its owner. In many places, for example Oberstdorf, Hindelang and Gunzesried, this annual event has developed into a folk festival with beer tents and lots of visitors.

## VIEHSCHEID

Sul circa 600 alpeggi, chiamati "Alpen" nell'Algovia, circa 30 000 pezzi di bestiame trascorrono l'estate. Se non ci sono stati incidenti nel tardo settembre si decorano le mucche e accompagnato dal suone di grosse campane si scende verso la valle fino alle piazza Scheideplatz, dove le mandrie vengono divise per proprietario. In molti post come Oberstdorf, Hindelang, Gunzesried la discesa dall'alpeggio è diventata una festa popolare con birrerie e moltissimi visitatori.

### SCHEIDEGG

Die Besiedelung des Gebietes um Scheidegg erfolgte zwischen dem 6. und 7. Jh. durch die Alemannen. Der Kneippkurort befindet sich auf dem Bergrücken des Pfänders in einer Höhenlage von 800 - 1.000 m. Diese Panorama-Höhenlage bietet einen großartigen Ausblick auf über 100 Gipfel der Alpen. Die Höhenlage bietet eine überdurchschnittliche Sonnenscheindauer und hervorragende Luftreinheitsverhältnisse, besonders im Winter. Schon Pfarrer Kneipp sagte: "Eine Winterkur ersetzt zwei Sommerkuren."

### SCHEIDEGG

The Scheidegg area was settled by Allemanians in the 6th and 7th centuries. The Kneipp spa is situated on the Pfänder ridge at a height of 800 – 1000 metres above sea level. This high-altitude location means there is a magnificent panoramic view of over 100 Alpine summits to be enjoyed, and also exceptional climatic conditions, with above-average sunshine, wonderfully clean air, especially in winter when, in the words of Pastor Kneipp, a spa health cure benefits you twice as much.

### SCHEIDEGG

La insediamento nella regione di Scheidegg avvenne tra il VI e il VII secolo con gli Alemanni. La stazione climatica Kneipp si trova sul dorso del monte Pfänder, tra il lago Bodensee e ad una Maltezza di 800-1000 m. Questa posizione panoramica offre una magnifica veduta su oltre 100 vette alpine e possiede una privilegiata esposizione solare al di sopra della media, oltre ad una eccellente purezza della Maria, particolarmente da Minverno; infatti, come soleva dire il reverendo Kneipp, an Una cura invernale sostituisce due estivevance.

**WANGEN / Allgäu, Altstadt mit Ravensburger Tor / Gate Ravensburg / La torre di Ravensburg**

Die mittelalterische Altstadt Wangens entspricht noch ganz der einstigen Freien Reichsstadt, noch bestehen weite Teile der Stadtmauer mit drei kunstvoll verzierten Tortürmen, schmückt manches historische Fachwerkhaus die winkeligen Gassen, lassen sich das frühbarocke Rathaus, die Martinskirche bewundern. Im Osten Wangens liegt die Großgemeinde Argenbühl in reizvoller, reichgegliederter Landschaft mit vielen Hügeln, Seen und der Alpenkulisse als Hintergrund. Hier findet man auch Ratzenried mit Schloß und Ruine.

The medieval old town of Wangen is just as it was as a free imperial town. Large parts of the town walls are still preserved, with three elaborately decorated gate-towers; historic old semi-timbered houses line the crooked little streets, the early baroque town hall and the fine church of St. Martin inviting you to tarry. The parish of Argenbühl to the east of Wangen is a charming, varied landscape with hills, lakes and the silhouette of the Alps as a backdrop. This is where Ratzenried is situated with its castle and ruins.

Il centro storico medievale di Wangen corresponde ancora oggi alla vecchia libera città dell'impero. Sono intere gran parti delle mura di città con tre torri decorati, ci sono molte case con intelaiatura rettangolare visibile nelle vecchie stradine, il municipio che risale al primo barocco e la chiesa di San Martino. A est di Wangen si trova il comune di Argenbühl in un paesaggio ricco di prati, colline, laghi e le Alpi nel fondo. Qui si trova anche Ratzenried con il suo castello e la rovina.

Das Städtchen Lindenberg liegt östlich vom Bodensee in 762 m Höhe. Dort oben herrscht bereits ein so rauhes Klima, daß es keine Obstgärten und Äcker mehr gibt, sondern Wiesen, Viehzucht und Milchwirtschaft dominieren wie fast überall im Allgäu. Deshalb gilt Lindenberg auch als „Käse-Zentrum". – Isny, im letzten südöstlichen Winkel des Württemberger Allgäus gelegen, zeigt mit seinen Gassen, der Stadtmauer, den Türmen und Toren und dem Kirchenbezirk in reizvoller Weise noch viele Elemente der einstigen Freien Reichsstadt.

The little town of Lindenberg in 762 metres above sea level east of the Lake Constance. Up here the climate is already so harsh that there are no orchards or fields of crops; meadows, dairy and cattle farming are predominant as almost every-where else in the Allgäu. Not surprisingly Lindenberg is considered a great cheese centre. – Isny, in the south-easternmost corner of the Württemberg part of the Allgäu, still retains many attractive features from its time as a free imperial town: the narrow streets, town walls, towers and gates, the area round the church.

Le cure climatiche e la cittadina Lindenberg (762) all'est Lago di Costanza. Lì il clima è già così rigido che non ci sono più frutteti o campi, ma prati, allevamento di bestiame e l'industria caseria dominano come del resto in tutta l'Algovia. Per questo motivo Lindenberg viene considerato il "centro del formaggio". – Isny, nell'estremo sud-est dell'Algovia mostra ancora oggi molti elementi della vecchia libera città dell'impero con le stradine strette, le mura di città, le torri e porte e l'area delle chiese.

## ALPSEE bei Immenstadt / Near Immenstadt / Vicino a Immenstadt

In ein freundlich-sanftes, sonnenreiches Bergtal knapp westlich von Immenstadt schmiegt sich der 3,4 km lange Alpsee, den alle schätzen – Badende, Bootsfahrer, Surfer usw. Um die Südostecke des Sees zieht sich der Ferienort Bühl, die anderen Ufer sind weitgehend unbebaut, im Westen findet man sogar Schilfzonen und feuchte Wiesen, die ein Vogelparadies bilden. Von den Hängen nördlich über dem See, etwa oberhalb von Trieblings, hat man einen besonders schönen Blick über die Wasserfläche auf die Allgäuer Berge.

The 3.4 km-long Alpsee, loved by bathers, boatsmen and surfers alike, nestles in a pleasant, gentle, sunny valley just west of Immenstadt. The resort of Bühl clusters round the southeastern corner of the lake, but the rest of the shoreline is for the most part not built on. To the west there are in fact areas of reeds and wetlands, a paradise for waterfowl. From the slopes to the north, up above the lake, for example above Trieblings, there is a particularly fine view across the water to the Allgäu mountains.

L'Alpsee, lungo 3,4 km si trova ad ovest di Immenstadt in una valle alpina molto soleggiata. Sia bagnanti che quelli in barca o con il surf ammirano questo lago. Nell'angolo meridionale del lago si trova il centro turistico Bühl, le altre rive sono ancora intoccate. Sulle rive occidentali ci sono adirittura zone di canne e prati umidi che offrono un paradiso per gli uccelli acquatici. Andando sulle colline a nord del lago, si ha una panoramica magnifica sul lago e le montagne dell'Algovia.

Burgruinen mit einer fast tausendjährigen Geschichte wie Hugofels, Rothenfels oder Laubenberg lassen die einstige strategische Bedeutung Immenstadts ahnen, das den Platz zwischen dem steilen Bergfuß, dem hier deutlich eingeschnittenen Tal der Iller und den Alpseen füllt. Der Marktplatz mit dem Marienbrunnen bildet noch heute den Mittelpunkt des „Städtle", wie die Einheimischen liebevoll sagen. Gleich jenseits der Iller liegt das Dorf Rauhenzell; die Pfarrkirche und das Schloss bilden ein schmuckes Ensemble.

Castle ruins with a history stretching back almost 1000 years, such as the Hugofels, Rothenfels or Laubenberg, are an indication of the once strategic importance of Immenstadt, filling as it does the space between the steep base of the mountain, the here quite deep valley of the Iller and the Alpsee. The marketplace with its fountain is still the focal point of the little town, "Städtle" as the locals lovingly call it. On the other side of the Iller is the village of Rauhenzell; the parish church and the castle are a neat little ensemble.

Rovine con una storia quasi millenaria sulle spalle come Hugofels, Rothenfels e Laubenberg danno una sensazione dell'importanza strategica che Immenstadt aveva nel passato. La città è situata nella valle del fiume Iller ed è circondata da monti ripidi e laghi della regione. La piazza del mercato con la fontana Marienbrunnen è ancora oggi il centro della cittadina, "Städtle" in dialetto locale. Al di là del fiume Iller si trova il paese Rauhenzell dove la chiesa parrocchiale e il castello formano un'insieme incantevole.

# KEMPTEN, Kloster und Kirche St. Lorenz / Monastery and church of St. Laurence / Convento e chiesa St- Lorenz

Mit gut 60.000 Einwohnern ist Kempten die Metropole des Allgäus, eine junge, lebendige Stadt mit sehr alter Geschichte, der Name geht sogar auf das keltische Cambodunum zurück. Ab 1289 bestanden hier unmittelbar nebeneinander eine Freie Reichsstadt, von der das sehenswerte Zentrum um das Rathaus und die St.-Mang-Kirche bis heute erhalten blieb, und ein geistlicher Bezirk, die Stiftsstadt. Die damaligen Fürstäbte ließen im 17. und 18. Jahrhundert das ausgedehnte Kloster und die Barockkirche St. Lorenz erbauen.

With a population of 60,000, Kempten is the "capital" of the Allgäu, a young town full of life but with a very long history, its name going back to Celtic Cambodunum, for example. From 1289 on, a free imperial town - the well worth-while centre round the town hall and the church of St. Mang have been preserved up to today - existed side by side with a separate clerical town under the rule of the church. The prince-abbots had the large monastery and baroque church built in the 17th and 18th centuries.

Con circa 60000 abitanti Kempten è la metropoli dell'Algovia, è una città molto giovanile e vivace con radici antichi in quanto il suo nome deriva dal nome celtico Cambodunum. A partire dal 1289 coesistevano da una parte la libera città dll'impero, di cui è testimone il centro storico attorno al municipio e la chiesa St.-Mang e dall'altra parte il quartiere religioso, dove si trova il convento. Gli abati principe fecero costruire l'ampio convento e la chiesa barocca St. Lorenz nel giro del 17. e 18. secolo.

## KEMPTEN, Orangerie im Hofgarten

Es lässt sich heute noch auf den ersten Blick die Zweiteilung der Stadt erkennen, es unterscheidet sich der geistliche Teil um das begüterte Reichsstift und der weltlich-reichsstädtische Teil um das Rathaus. 1527 wurde die Stadt protestantisch, mitten drin das katholische Reichsstift. Erst die Säkularisation verband die Stadt zu einer Einheit. – Das filigrane Gebäude der Orangerie wurde 1780 als nördlicher Abschluss des ursprünglich in drei Terrassen angelegten Hofgartens erstellt und dient heute als Bibliothek.

The division of the town into two separate parts is still visible today – the spiritual part round the well-to-do imperial religious foundation, and the secular imperial city part centred round the town hall. In 1527 the town became Protestant, hence the Catholic foundation. Secularization finally reunited the town as one entity. – The filigree Orangery building was completed in 1780 as the northern end of the Court Garden, originally laid out as three terraces. Today it houses the library.

Ancor oggi si distingue al primo sguardo la ripartizione della città in due parti: la parte religiosa è quella raccolta attorno al facoltoso convento, quella laico-imperiale attorno al municipio. Nel 1527 la città si convertì al protestantesimo, e così il convento cattolico divenne un vicino scomodo. Solo dopo la secolarizzazione la città fu riunificata. – L'edificio a filigrana dell'aranceria, fu eretto nel 1780 al confine settentrionale del giardino di corte, che originalmente si estendeva su tre terrazze, e oggi funge da biblioteca.

**KEMPTEN**, Barock-Kirche St. Lorenz

Die Basilika St. Lorenz, errichtet 1652 bis 1666, ist der erste große Kirchenbau nördlich der Alpen nach dem Dreißigjährigen Krieg. Schon hier wird das Lichte und Fröhliche spürbar, das später den eigentlichen Zauber des süddeutschen Barock und Rokoko ausmacht.

**KEMPTEN**, Basilica of St. Laurence

The basilica of St. Laurence, built between 1652 and 1656, is the first great sacred building to be constructed north of the Alps after the Thirty Years War. One can sense the light cheerfulness that was to form the real charm of the south-German baroque and rococo.

**KEMPTEN**, Chiesa St. Lorenz

La basilica St. Lorenz, costruita dal 1652 al 1666, è la prima costruzione ecclesiastica al nord delle Alpi dopo la guerra dei trent'anni. Già in questa chiesa si sente la leggerezza e la luce che renderanno famosi il barocco e il rococò della Germania meridionale.

# KEMPTEN, Residenz

Keine weltlichen Fürsten, sondern Äbte schufen die gewaltige Residenz in Kempten. Die schlichten Fassaden lassen wenig vom prunkvollen Inneren ahnen. Berühmte Künstler, etwa Üblherr und die Brüder Zimmermann, schmückten die Räume wie das „Tagzimmer" aus.

# KEMPTEN, Residence

It was not secular dukes, but abbots who created the magnificent residence in Kempten. The simple facades give no inkling of the sumptuous interior. Famous artists and craftsmen, such as Üblherr and the Zimmermann brothers decorated rooms like the "Tagzimmer".

# KEMPTEN, Residenza

Non erano principi laici, ma abati che fecereo costruire la residenza imponente di Kempten. Le facciate semplici non danno nessun segno dell'interno sfarzoso. Artisti famosi come Übelherr e i fratelli Zimmermann decorarono le sale come per esempio il soggiorno "Tagzimmer".

# KEMPTEN, Rathaus

1368 wurde das Rathaus, die damalige Kornschranne erst als Fachwerkbau, 1474 dann als Steinbau errichtet.

# KEMPTEN, town hall

The town hall was built in 1368, first as a timbered granary, the stone building following in 1474.

# KEMPTEN, il municipio

Nel 1368 il municipio, l'allora granaio, fu costruito come edificio a travatura, e nel 1474 in pietra.

## MARIA STEINBACH / Iller, Wallfahrtskirche / Pilgrimage church / Chiesa santuaria

Zu Maria Steinbach im „Illerwinkel" gehört ein barockes Juwel, das sich abseits aller üblichen Wege versteckt. Ein besonders stimmungsvoller Zugang: von Wagsberg bei Illerbeuren mit der Fähre über die Iller und zu Fuß in 15 Minuten hinauf zum 400-Seelen-Dorf Maria Steinbach und zur Wallfahrtskirche von 1753. Sie ist von Benedikt Stadelhofer in Anlehnung an die Architektur von Dominikus Zimmermann geplant worden. Den feinen, lebendigen Rokoko-Stuck schuf Johann Georg Üblherr als seine letzte und vielleicht reifste Arbeit.

Maria Steinbach at the "Illerwinkel" is the home of a baroque gem, hidden away off the beaten track. A particularly idyllic way of approaching it is by ferry across the Iller and then on foot up through the 400-strong village of Maria Steinbach to the pilgrimage church of 1753. It was designed by Benedikt Stadelhofer incorporating ideas of the architect Dominkus Zimmermann. The fine, lively rococo stuccowork is by Johann Georg Üblherr, his last and perhaps most mature creation.

Maria Steinbach dell'Illerwinkel, un'altro gioiello barocco che si nasconde al di là dei cammini normali. Un accesso molto bello è da Wagsberg vicino a Illerbeuren con il traghetto fino all'altra riva della Iller e poi 15 minuti a piedi fino al paese Maria Steinbach che comprende 400 abitanti. Lì si trova il santuario del 1753. E stato progettato da Benedikt Stadelhofer basandosi sull'architettuta di Dominikus Zimmermann. I lavori di stucco barocco sono stati fatti da Johann Georg Übelherr, la sua ultima e forse più matura opera.

### Barock-Kirche „Maria Steinbach"

**MEMMINGEN, Marktplatz mit Rathaus / Marketplace and town hall / Piazza del mercato**

Die Altstadt Memmingens zeigt noch ganz die Anlage der einstigen Reichsstadt, noch stehen zwei Drittel der Stadtmauern, je fünf Tore und Türme, fließt der Stadtbach. Um den weiten Markplatz gruppieren sich das Rathaus, eine Symbiose aus Renaissance und Rokoko, das Steuerhaus von 1495 und die mächtige gotische Martinskirche. In der Lindentorstraße ragt schmal und hoch das Siebendächerhaus auf. Und 10 km weiter östlich wartet eine weitere Kostbarkeit, die Basilika der ehemaligen Benediktiner-Abtei von Ottobeuren.

The old town of Memmingen is still very much the former imperial town that it once was. Two thirds of the old town walls, five gates and towers are still standing, the stream still flows through the streets. Set out around the broad marketplace are the town hall, a symbiosis of the Renaissance and rococo, the tax building of 1495 and the mighty Gothic church of St. Martin. The "house of the seven roofs" rises up tall and narrow in the Lindentorstraße. And ten kilometres to the east a further treasure awaits the visitor, the basilica of Ottobeuren.

Il centro storico di Memmingen corrisponde esattamente a quello della vecchia libera città dell'impero, ci sono ancora due terzi delle mura, cinque torri e cinque porte nonché anche il ruscello della città. Attorno all'ampia piazza del mercato si trovano il municipio, una simbiosi tra rinascimento e rococò, il Steuerhaus del 1495 e l'imponente chiesa di San Martino. Nella Lindentorsraße si trova la casa dei sette tetti, Siebendächerhaus. A 10 chilometri ad est incontriamo un altro gioiello, la basilica di Ottobeuren.

**OTTOBEUREN, Basilika**

Noch mehr als die Benediktiner-Abtei beeindruckt die stolz über dem Markplatz thronende Basilika die Besucher. Viele der berühmtesten Künstler wie der Baumeister Johann Michael Fischer, der Stukkateur Johann Michael Feichtmayr oder der Maler Johann Jakob Zeiller arbeiteten Hand in Hand an dieser prachtvollen Rokoko-Kirche, die 1766 geweiht wurde. Die beiden Barockorgeln und der herrliche Innenraum mögen die Ottobeurer Konzerte angeregt haben, Veranstaltungen, die von Kunstfreunden sehr geschätzt werden.

Even more impressive than the Benedictine abbey is the basilica towering up over the marketplace. Many of the most famous artists of the period, including the architect Johann Michael Fischer, the stuccoworker Johann Michael Feichtmayr or the painter Johann Jakob Zeller, worked hand in hand to create this magnificent rococo church, consecrated in 1766. The two baroque organs and the splendid interior may well have inspired the Ottobeuren concerts, cultural events greatly valued by music-lovers.

Più imponente del convento si presenta la basilica di Ottobeuren, che si trova sopra la piazza del mercato. Molti artisti conosciuti in tutto il mondo collaborarono alle costruzione della basilica rococò consacrata nel 1766. Tra di loro ci furono l'architetto Johann Michael Fischer, lo stuccatore Johann Michael Feichtmayr e il pittore Johann Jakob Zeiller. I due organi barocchi e l'interno magnifico hanno dato l'idea dei concerti di Ottobeuren, manifestazioni molto pregiati da amici della musica.

## OTTOBEUREN, Abtei-Bibliothek / Library in the abbey / Biblioteca nell'abbazia

Stephansried heißt ein Dörfchen im Unterallgäu; 1821 kam dort Sebastian Kneipp zur Welt. Das brachte und bringt dem nur wenige Kilometer entfernten Ottobeuren seine Bedeutung als Kneipp-Kurort. Doch ungleich berühmter wurde der Ort durch die Bauten der Benediktiner im 18. Jahrhundert. Hier entstand die größte und wohl prachtvollste Klosteranlage Süddeutschlands mit einem Hauptgebäude von 140 x 125 m. Kunstvoll ausgestaltet sind die Treppenhäuser, Säle und die Bibliothek mit ihren 15000 in ledergebundenen alten Bänden.

Stephansried is a small village in the Lower Allgäu and the birthplace of Sebastian Kneipp. Hence the reputation of Ottobeuren, only a few kilometres away, as a Kneipp spa. The town's fame stems, however, to a much greater degree from the buildings erected by the Benedictines in the 18th century. This is the site of the largest and probably finest monastery complex in the whole of Southern Germany with its 140 x 125 m large main building. The staircases, halls and the library with its 15000 volumes bound in leather are all elaborately decorated.

Stephansried, ecco il nome di un paesino nell'Algovia dove nel 1821 è nato Sebastian Kneipp. Questo fatto ha contribuito e contribuisce ancora alla fama di Ottobeuren come bagno di cure Kneipp. Ma è più conosciuto per le costruzioni dei benedettini nel 18. secolo. In questo periodo fu costruito il convento più grande in tutta la Germania meridionale. L'edificio maggiore è di 140 x 125 metri. Particolarmente decorate sono le scale, le sale e la biblioteca che comprende 15000 volumi legati in pelle.

### IRSEE, Barockkirche, Schiffskanzel

Auf den Höhen im Nordwesten Kaufbeurens verstecken sich der Markt Irsee (774 m) und ein einstiges Benediktinerkloster. Zu ihm gehört eine reizvolle Barockkirche, die eine Schiffskanzel beherbergt, die an die Seeschlacht von Lepanto (1571) – den Sieg des Christentums über den Islam – erinnert.

### IRSEE, Baroque church, ship´s pulpit

Irsee (774m) with its former Benedictine monastery lies tucked away in the hills to the northwest of Kaufbeuren. Part of the complex is a fine baroque church with a pulpit in the form of a ship, in memory of the naval battle of Lepanto (1571) when Christianty triumphed over Islam.

### IRSEE, Chiesa barocca, pulpito navale

Sulle colline a nord-ovest di Kaufbeuren si nasconde il Markt Irsee (774m) e un vecchio convento benedettino. Di questo fa parte un'incantevole chiesa barocca che ospita un pulpito a forma di nave che ricorda la battaglia navale di Lepanto (1571) - la vittoria del cristianesimo sull'islam.

### KAUFBEUREN, Altstadt

Die Altstadt Kaufbeurens zeigt noch die Anlage der ehemaligen Freien Reichsstadt; manche historische Fassade erinnert an jene Zeit. Und über den Dächern ragen drei Türme und ein Teil der Stadtmauer auf, in die das gotische Blasius-Kirchlein mit wertvollem Lederer-Schnitzaltar eingebaut ist.

The design of the old free imperial town is still visible in the old town of Kaufbeuren; many a historic facade reminds us of that period. Rising up above the town are three towers and part of the town wall, housing the little Gothic Blasius church with a precious altar by Lederer.

Il centro storico di Kaufbeuren ha conservato le strutture della vecchia libera città dell'impero, alcune facciate storiche fanno ricordare il passato. Sopra i tetti si vedono tre torri e parti delle mura di città nelle quali è costruita la chiesa gotica Blasius-Kirchlein con il prezioso altare di Lederer rifinito in legno.

## MINDELHEIM, Blick von der Mindelburg — MARKTOBERDORF an der Wertach im Ostallgäu

Die Altstadt mit ihren Türmen, Toren, Kirchen und dem Kloster läßt ein wenig von der reichen geschichtlichen Vergangenheit Mindelheims ahnen, das im Laufe der Zeit den Welfen, Staufern, Teck, Rechberg, Bayern, Fugger gehörte, und natürlich den Frundsberg, an die zudem die sauber renovierte Mindelburg erinnert. – Im Süden von Kaufbeuren trifft man bald auf die Kreisstadt Marktoberdorf. In beherrschender Lage auf dem Schloßberg steht deren barocke Pfarrkirche, ein meisterliches Werk des Einheimischen Johann Georg Fischer, der auch das Jagdschloß schuf.

The old town with its towers, gates, churches and monastery gives us an idea of the rich historical past of Mindelheim, which, at different periods, was ruled by the Welfen, Staufer, Teck, Rechberg, Bavaria, the Fugger, and of course the Frundsberg, whom we are reminded of by the smartly renovated Mindelburg. – Not far south of Kaufbeuren is the district town of Marktoberdorf. In a dominant position up on the castle hill is the baroque parish church, a magnificent building by the local architect Johann Georg Fischer.

Il centro storico con le sue torri, porte, chiese e il suo convento da una piccola impressione del ricco passato storico di Mindelheim che nel corso dei secoli apparteneva ai guelfi, agli Hohenstaufer, Teck, Rechberg, bavaresi e Fugger e naturalmente ai Frundsberg che hanno restaurato il castello Mindelburg. – Andando a sud di Kaufbeuren si arriva al comune di Kaufbeuren. In una posizione dominante sul Schloßberg si trova la barocca chiesa parroc-chiale, un'opera magnifica dell'architetto locale Johann Georg Fischer che costruise anche il castello di caccia, Jagdschloß.

## STEINGADEN im Pfaffenwinkel

Den Bergen schon nahe und am Rande des Pfaffenwinkels gelegen steht bei dem Ort Steingaden die Wieskirche. Hier stellt man sich verwundert die Frage, welcher Anlaß es wohl gewesen sein mag, in einer so einsamen Gegend ein so ungewöhnlich prachtvolles Gotteshaus zu errichten. In der Tat hat sich hier Außergewöhnliches in mehrerlei Hinsicht ereignet: Tränen, ein urmenschliches Phänomen, sind hier gleichsam zu geistigen Bausteinen, zu kostbaren Perlen geworden, aus denen das weltberühmte Rokokojuwel, die Wieskirche, erstand.

The Wieskirche lies close by the mountains, on the edge of the Pfaffenwinkel. As you stand and gaze, you can't help but wonder what could have induced the building of such a uniquely magnificent place of worship in such a lonely region. And indeed this is the scene of unusual events: heartbreak, an inhuman phenomenon became, as it were, transfigured and turned into spiritual building blocks, precious pearls that gave birth to the world-famous rococo gem, the Wieskirche.

A ridosso dei monti e ai margini del Pfaffenwinkel si trova la Wieskirche. Qui ci si chiede meravigliati, quale occasione abbia spinto a costruire una chiesa così insolitamente sontuosa in un posto talmente isolato. In effetti qui lo straordinario si è espresso sotto molti aspetti: le lacrime, un fenomeno prettamente umano, sono qui diventate mattoni spirituali, perle preziose di cui è fatta la Wieskirche, famoso gioiello del Rococò.

## WIESKIRCHE bei Steingaden

Sie wurde zum Ort der Verehrung des Gegeißelten Heilandes im 18.Jh., schon damals europaweit bekannt und als Kleinod barocker Baukunst gerühmt. Die Wieskirche ist ein Werk des Wessobrunner Baumeisters Dominikus Zimmermann und entstand um 1750. Den lichtdurchfluteten Innenraum statteten die berühmtesten süddeutschen Stukkateure und Maler jener Zeit aus. Aus diesen beiden Quellen - ihrem geistlichen wie künstlerischen Reichtum - lebt die Wies bis heute: Sie ist seit ihrer Entstehung Wallfahrtsstätte.

## WIESKIRCHE near Steingaden

It became a place of pilgrimage and homage to the Chastised Saviour in the 18th century, when it was already famous and known all over Europe as a gem of baroque architecture. The Wieskirche was created by the Wessobrunn architect Dominkus Zimmermann and built around 1750. The interior, bathed in light, was decorated by the most distinguished stucco-workers and painters of the period in Southern Germany. The Wieskirche still draws its lifeblood from these two sources today, its spiritual and artistic wealth. It has been a place of pilgrimage since its creation.

## La chiesa WIESKIRCHE

La chiesa divenne famosa già nel XVIII secolo in tutta Europa come luogo di adorazione del Cristo flagellato e come gemma dell'architettura barocca. La Wieskirche è opera dell'architetto di Wessobrunn Dominikus Zimmermann, e sorse attorno al 1750. Gli interni luminosissimi furono addobbati dai più famosi stuccatori e pittori della Germania meridionale dell'epoca. Di queste due fonti - la sua ricchezza spirituale e artistica - vive tuttora la Wieskirche: essa è meta di pellegrinaggio sin dalla sua nascita.from these two sources today, its spiritual and artistic wealth. It has been a place of pilgrimage since its creation.

WIESKIRCHE bei Steingaden ▷▷